CAMBRIDGE PRIMARY
Mathematics

Learner's Book

1

Cherri Moseley and Janet Rees

CAMBRIDGE
UNIVERSITY PRESS

University Printing House, Cambridge CB2 8BS, United Kingdom

Cambridge University Press is part of the University of Cambridge.

It furthers the University's mission by disseminating knowledge in the pursuit of education, learning and research at the highest international levels of excellence.

Information on this title: education.cambridge.org

© Cambridge University Press 2014

First published 2014
10th printing 2016

Printed in Spain by GraphyCems

A catalogue record for this publication is available from the British Library

ISBN 978-1-107-63131-1 Paperback

....

....

The authors and publishers acknowledge the following sources of copyright material and are grateful for the permissions granted. While every effort has been made, it has not always been possible to identify the sources of all the material used, or to trace all copyright holders. If any omissions are brought to our notice, we will be happy to include the appropriate acknowledgements on reprinting.

PHOTOGRAPHS

pp. 11*t,b*, 84 Janet Rees; p. 23*tl* kmt_rf/Alamy; p. 23*tr* danako/Alamy; p. 23*bl* Melinda Fawver/Thinkstock; p. 23*br* Dvpdt/Shutterstock; p. 46*tl* Trimages/Thinkstock; p. 46*tr* GrÃ§a Victoria/Thinkstock; p. 46*cl* aerogondo/Thinkstock; p. 46*cr* Kasper Christiansen/Thinkstock; p. 46*bl* Getty Images/Thinkstock; p. 46*bc* Sergey Galushko/Thinkstock; p. 46*br* studioraffi/Thinkstock; p. 55*tl* BananaStock/Thinkstock; p. 55*tr* ChrisPole/Thikstock; p. 55*bl* Chad Davis/Thinkstock; p. 55 *br* DNHanlon/Thinkstock; p. 78*tl* Baloncici/Thinkstock; p. 78*tr* vora/Thinkstock; p. 78*bl* Claus Mikosch/Thinkstock; p. 78*br* Keith Levitt/Thinkstock

t = top *c* = centre *b* = bottom *l* = left *r* = right

Introduction

This *Learner's Book* is a supplementary resource that consolidates and reinforces mathematical learning alongside the *Cambridge Primary Mathematics Teacher's Resource 1* (9781107656833). It acts as a useful consolidation tool for the learners by providing points for discussion to develop problem-solving skills and support learning through discovery and discussion. Rote learning and drill exercises are avoided.

Ideally, a session should be taught using the appropriate *Core activity* in the *Teacher's Resource 1*, with the *Learner's Book* page open during the session as a visual reference and/or guide for the learner. There are sometimes simple questions or activities that could be used to assess learner understanding. There is a single page corresponding to each *Core activity* in the *Teacher's Resource 1* printed book. The *Core activity* that the page relates to is indicated at the bottom of the page.

Hints and tips are provided throughout to support the learners. They will appear as follows:

> Write a list of number pairs to help you

Please note that the *Learner's Book* on its own does not cover all of the Cambridge Primary mathematics curriculum framework for Stage 1. It needs to be used in conjunction with the *Teacher's Resource 1*. The *Teacher's Resource 1* and *Learner's Book 1* do not follow the order of the Cambridge Primary mathematics curriculum framework. Although all of the objectives in the framework are covered, they are approached in a different order.

This publication is part of the *Cambridge Primary Maths* project. *Cambridge Primary Maths* is an innovative combination of curriculum and resources designed to support teachers and learners to succeed in primary mathematics through best-practice international maths teaching and a problem-solving approach.

Cambridge Primary Maths brings together the world-class Cambridge Primary mathematics curriculum from Cambridge International Examinations, high-quality publishing from Cambridge University Press and expertise in engaging online enrichment materials for the mathematics curriculum from NRICH. Teachers have access to an online tool that maps resources and links to materials offered through the primary mathematics curriculum, NRICH and Cambridge Primary mathematics textbooks and e-books. These resources include engaging online activities, best-practice guidance and examples of *Cambridge Primary Maths* in action.

The Cambridge curriculum is dedicated to helping schools develop learners who are confident, responsible, reflective, innovative and engaged. It is designed to give learners the skills to problem solve effectively, apply mathematical knowledge and develop a holistic understanding of the subject.

The *Cambridge Primary Maths* textbooks provide best-in-class support for this problem-solving approach, based on pedagogical practice found in successful schools across the world. The engaging NRICH online resources help develop mathematical thinking and problem-solving skills. To get involved visit www.cie.org.uk/cambridgeprimarymaths

The benefits of being part of *Cambridge Primary Maths* are:

- the opportunity to explore a maths curriculum founded on the values of the University of Cambridge and best practice in schools
- access to an innovative package of online and print resources that can help bring the Cambridge Primary mathematics curriculum to life in the classroom.

This series is arranged to ensure that the curriculum is covered whilst allowing teachers to use a flexible approach. The Scheme of Work for Stage 1 has been followed, though there are a few deviations. The components are:

- Teacher's Resource 1 ISBN: 9781107656833 (printed book and CD-ROM).
- Learner's Book 1 ISBN: 9781107631311 (printed book)
- Games Book 1 ISBN: 9781107646407 (printed book and CD-ROM).

Numbers

Unit 1A Core activity 1.1 Recognising and saying numbers up to ten

Up to Ten

How many?

How many in each group?

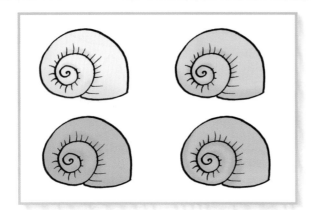

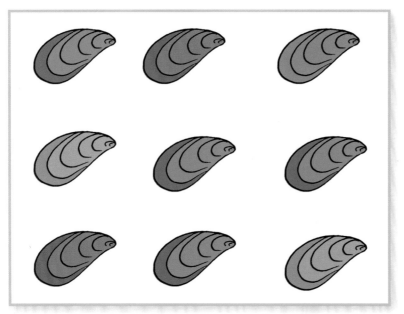

Vocabulary

count

How many?

1, 2, ...

4

count

How many?

count

1, 2, ...

5

5

Make ten

Find two numbers to make ten.

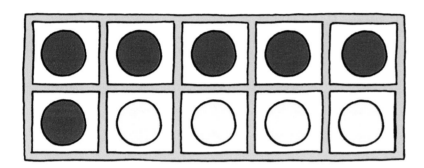

Find three numbers to make ten.

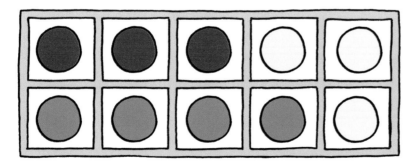

Ten take away

How many are there left?

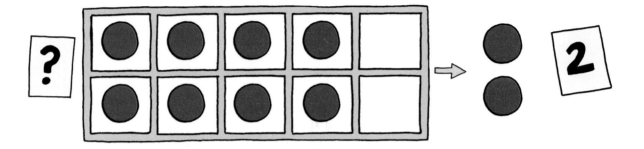

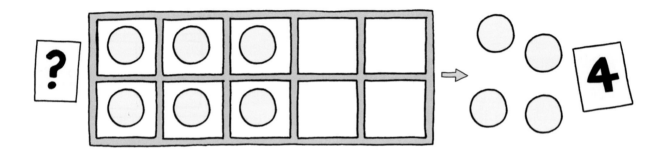

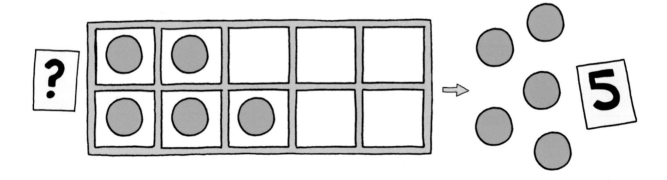

Doubles

Double 1 makes 2.

Vocabulary

double

Double 2 makes 4.

What other doubles can you find?

Giant footprints

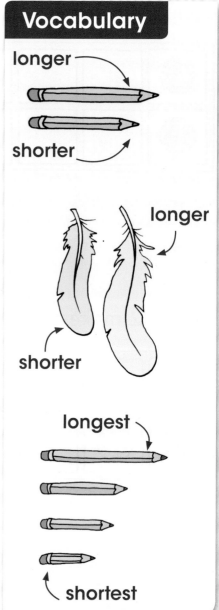

Vocabulary

longer

shorter

longer

shorter

longest

shortest

How long is your footprint?

How long is the giant's footprint?

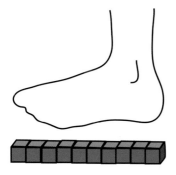

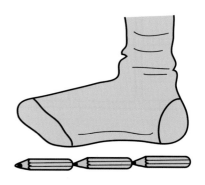

Height

Which is taller? The ice cream or the boy?

Which is tallest? The lady or the buildings?

Number pairs

This is a number pair for .

Vocabulary

number pairs:

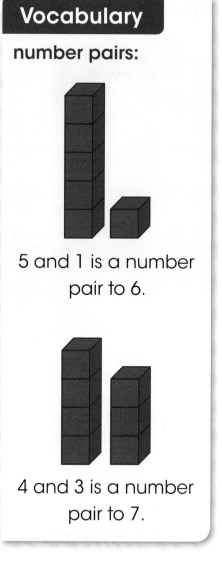

5 and 1 is a number pair to 6.

4 and 3 is a number pair to 7.

This is a number pair for .

This is a number pair for . This is a number pair for ? .

Oh no!

Write the teen numbers in the correct order.

Vocabulary

teen numbers: all the numbers that are made of ten and some ones.

Use a number track to help you.

10									20

Estimate and count

Vocabulary

estimate:

count:

How many?

1	2	3	4	5	6	7	8	9	10
11	12	13	14	15	16	17	18	19	20
21	22	23	24	25	26	27	28	29	30

Twice as many?

How many?

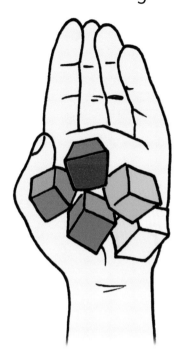

Is this twice as many?

How do you know?

Vocabulary

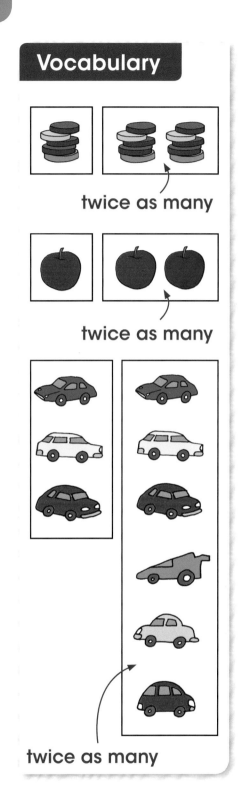

twice as many

twice as many

twice as many

What is the shape?

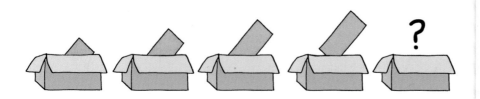

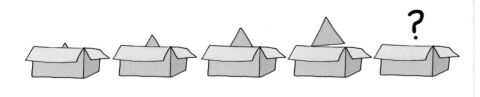

Making four squares

You will need:

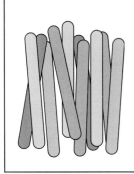
sticks

a pencil or chalk

a dice

Vocabulary

square

pentagon

hexagon

5

dice

You can draw the squares too.

You could make or draw other shapes.

triangle

pentagon

hexagon

Solids

What solids can you make by putting these 2D shapes together?

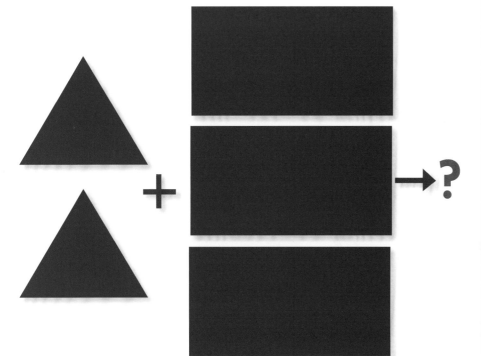

Vocabulary

cube

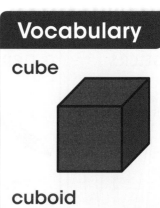

cuboid

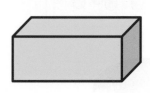

sphere

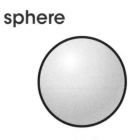

cone

pyramid

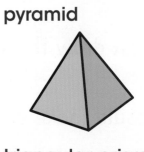

triangular prism

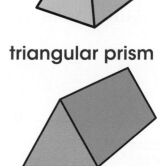

Unit 1B Core activity 6.2 3D solids

What is next?

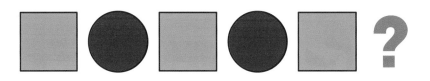 ?

Vocabulary

pattern

 ?

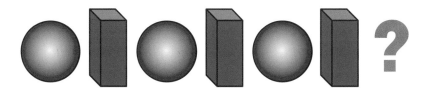 ?

 ?

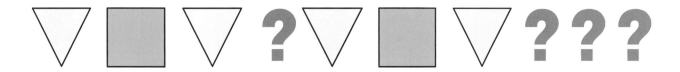

Symmetry and patterns

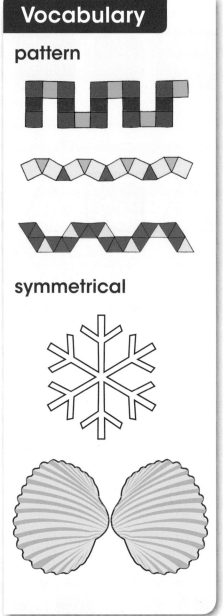

symmetrical

Unit 1B Core activity 6.3 Symmetry and patterns

Jigsaws

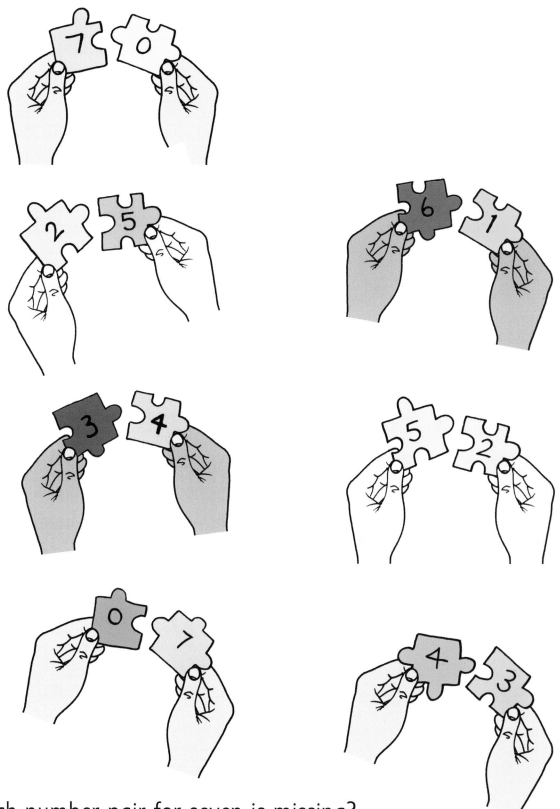

Which number pair for seven is missing?
Find the number pairs that are the same.

The 100 square

What number patterns can you see in the 100 square?

1	2	3	4	5	6	7	8	9	10
11	12	13	14	15	16	17	18	19	20
21	22	23	24	25	26	27	28	29	30
31	32	33	34	35	36	37	38	39	40
41	42	43	44	45	46	47	48	49	50
51	52	53	54	55	56	57	58	59	60
61	62	63	64	65	66	67	68	69	70
71	72	73	74	75	76	77	78	79	80
81	82	83	84	85	86	87	88	89	90
91	92	93	94	95	96	97	98	99	100

Capacity

Look at these pictures:

Ordering capacity

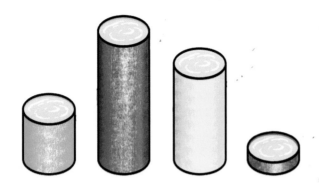

Vocabulary

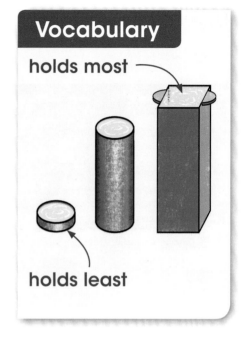

holds most

holds least

Which holds most?

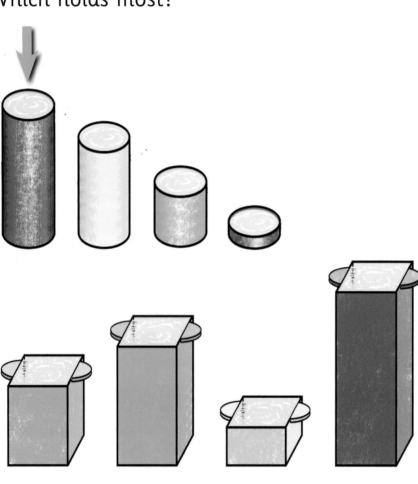

Which holds least?

? ? ?

Class café

What food will the café sell?

Make a menu to show the food.
The menu can be any shape.

The menu can be large.

The menu can be small.

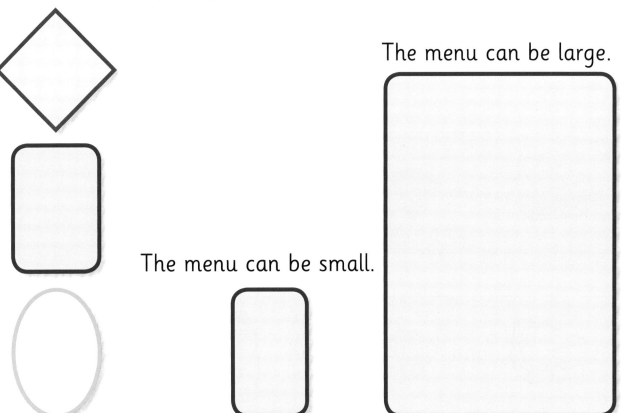

What is the price?

How much do these cost in your café?

How much do these meals cost in your café?

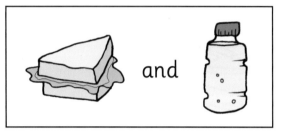

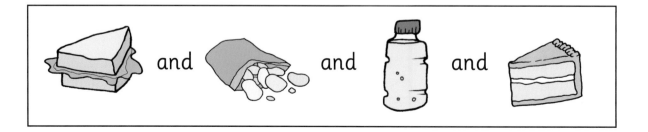

Unit 1C Core activity 9.2 Money

Our classroom café

We are open in the morning
We open at 11 o'clock

We serve lunch at 12 o'clock
We stop serving lunch at
2 o'clock

We serve tea at 3 o'clock
for 1 hour
We close in the afternoon
We close at 4 o'clock

Café opening times

Make a poster to show when the café is open.

Your poster can be any shape.

Our classroom café

Your poster can be big.

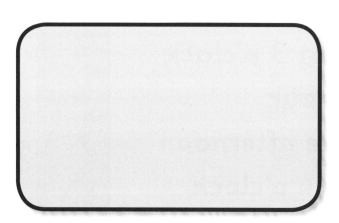

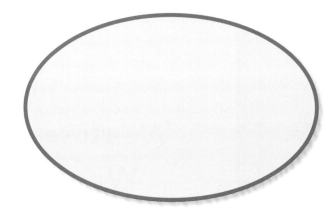

Your poster can be small.

Heavier and lighter

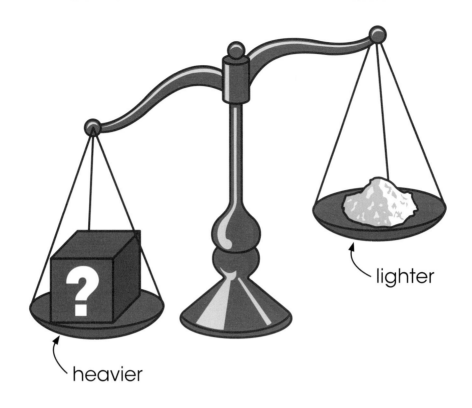

lighter

heavier

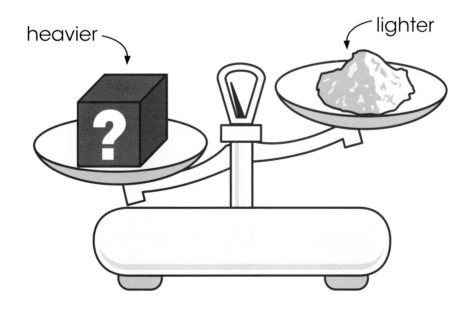

heavier

lighter

Heavier than, lighter than

heavier   lighter

What is heavier than the apple?

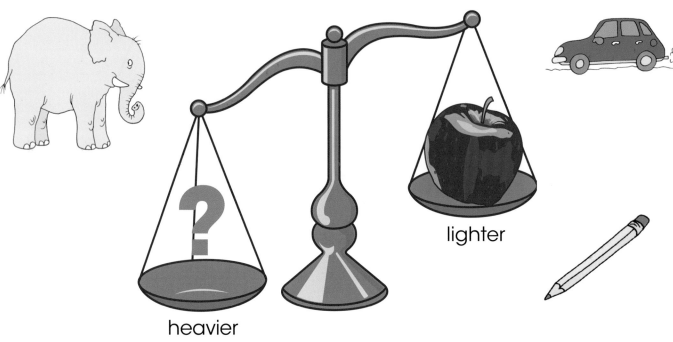

heavier   lighter

What is lighter than the apple?

lighter   heavier

Unit 1C Core activity 10.1 Direct comparison

Using a bucket balance

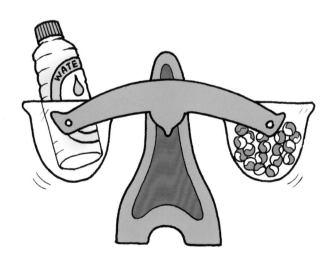

Pairs

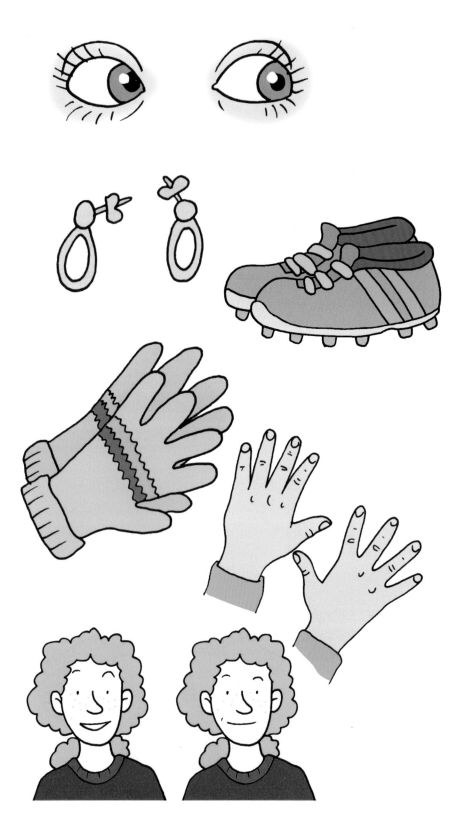

Can you think of any other pairs?

pair:

even numbers:

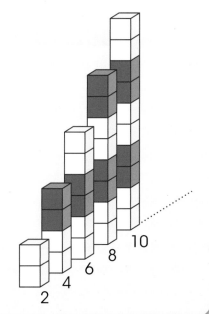

2 4 6 8 10

Odd numbers

odd numbers:

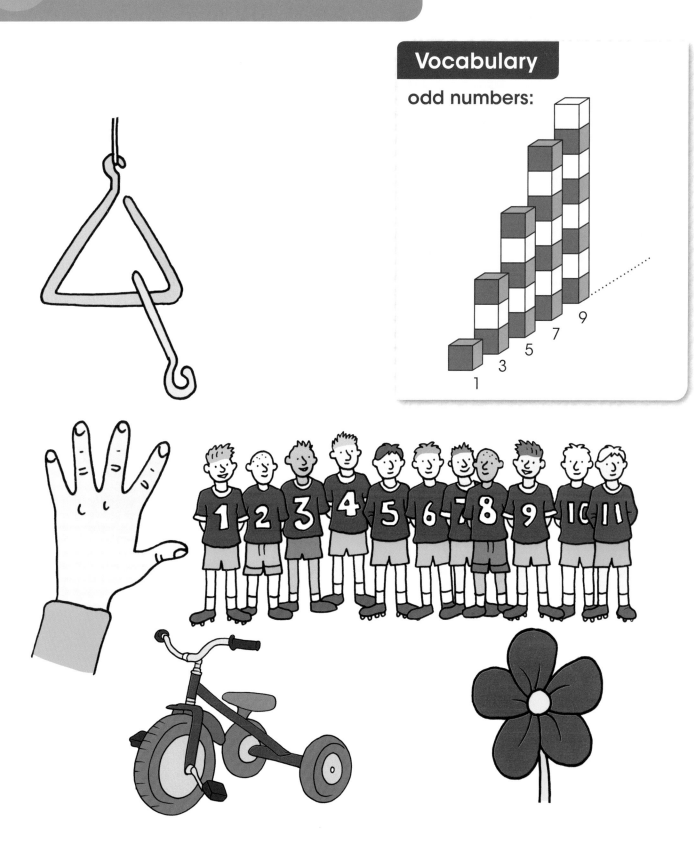

Can you think of anything else that comes in an odd number?

Odd or even?

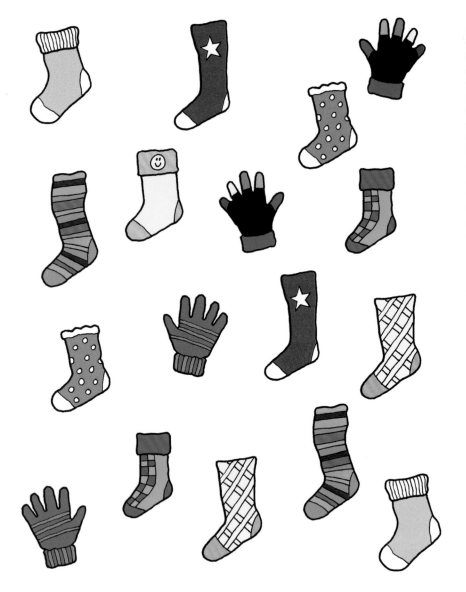

Vocabulary

sock

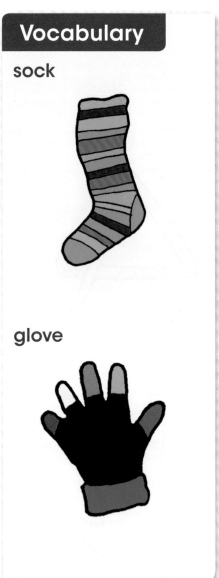

glove

How many socks can you see?

Is that an odd number or an even number?

How many gloves can you see?

Is that an odd number or an even number?

How many socks and gloves altogether?

Is that an odd number or an even number?

Numbers in order

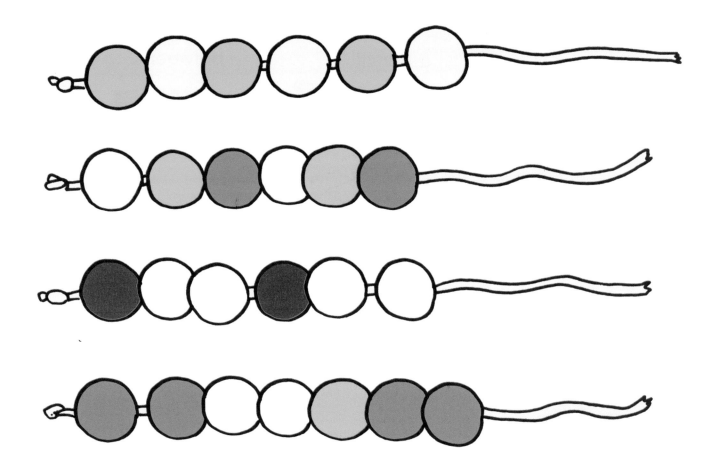

For each string of beads:

What colour will the 7th bead be?

What colour will the 11th bead be?

What colour will the 17th bead be?

What colour will the 10th bead be?

Between

You will need:

four dice

a pencil

and some paper

Vocabulary

between

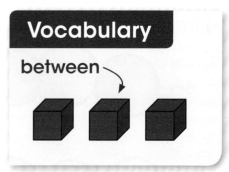

Which numbers are between 13 and 21?

13   21

More than Ten

What is the total for each group of balloons?

total

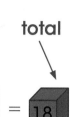

$6 + 4 + 8 = 18$

6 2 4

3 7 4

6 5 5

Use number pairs to 10 to help you.

3 8 5

2 8 7

9 8 1

Fields

Find the total of two pots.

Shut the gate!

Number Lines

Find the difference.

find the difference

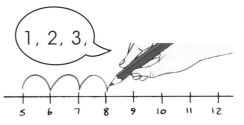

The difference between 5 and 8 is 3.

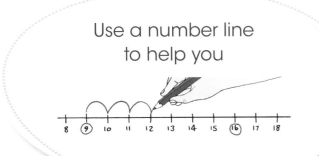

Use a number line to help you

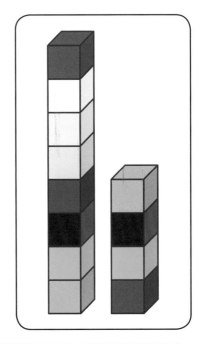

Jump back two

Roberto jumps back two.
Which number does he land on?

| 11 | 12 | 13 | 14 | 15 | 16 | | 18 | 19 |

Use a number line to help you

8 9 10 11 12 13 14 15 16 17 18 19 20

Unit 2A Core activity 13.5 Number line (2) adding and subtracting two

Shoe stack

Which is the smallest shoe size?

Which is the biggest shoe size?

Vocabulary

Shoe size

Write the shoe sizes in order.

Ice cream flavours

You can buy two scoops of ice cream.
How many different ice creams can you make?

What is money?

How can you make the amount you need to buy:

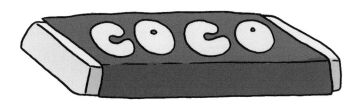

a chocolate bar?

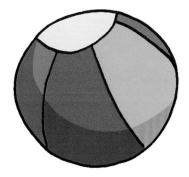

a ball?

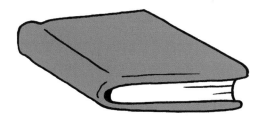

a book?

an ice cream?

Our class shop

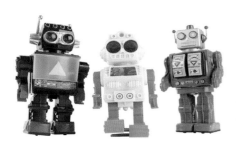

Ordering length

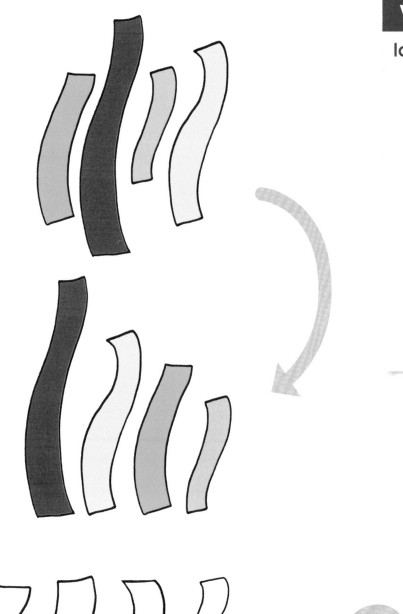

Vocabulary

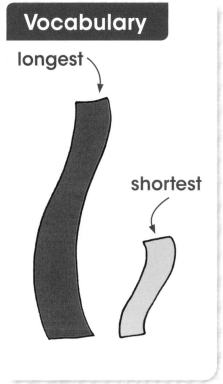

longest

shortest

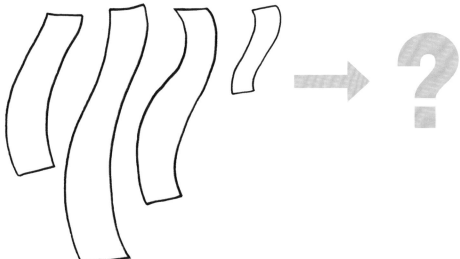

Vocabulary

tallest

shortest

Ordering weight

Vocabulary

lightest

heaviest

Put these objects in order of lightest to heaviest.

Balancing weight

Capacity (1)

How many things can you hold in your hand?

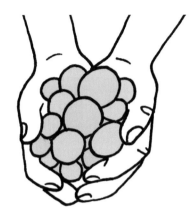

Vocabulary

capacity is 8 marbles

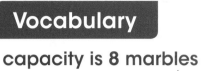

capacity is 10 cubes

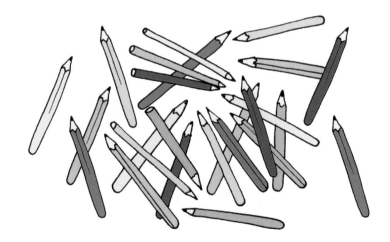

Draw the thing you held.

Write the capacity of your hands next to each drawing.

Capacity (2)

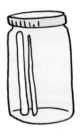   

Time

"I can catch a ball 12 times in one minute."

one minute

What can you do in one minute?

Count and record.
You can draw pictures of your activity or
write what you have done.

My day

What do you do on Monday?
What do you do on Saturday?
What if you go on holiday?

What if you go on a visit?
Will your day be the same?
What will be the same and what will
be different?

Vocabulary

Monday, Tuesday,

Wednesday,

Thursday, Friday

Saturday, Sunday

Months of the year

January, February, March, April, May, June, July, August, September, October, November, December.

Choose a month. Draw something that happens in that month.

Sorting into groups

Sort the months into the correct group.

Hot	Cold
Dry	**Rainy**

June

September

December

May

January

October

April

November

February

August

March

July

What is the rule?

What are the rules?

Ice cream pictogram

How many people like each flavour of ice cream?

chocolate   vanilla   strawberry   mint

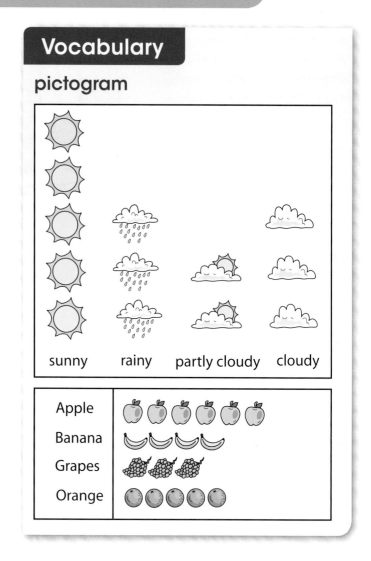

How many people like chocolate ice cream?

How many people like vanilla ice cream?

How many people like strawberry ice cream?

How many people like mint ice cream?

Draw the ice cream you like best.

Favourite meal time block graph

Favourite meal time.

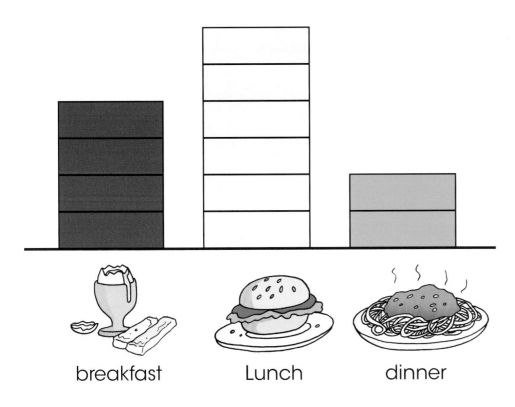

How many people like breakfast?

How many people like lunch?

How many people like dinner?

Sorting

Close your eyes and pick up ten cubes.

Vocabulary

Venn diagram

Open your eyes and sort them onto the
Venn diagram.

red

not red

How many red cubes?
How many not red cubes?

Sorting shapes

You will need a set of shapes.

Pick up eight shapes.
Sort the shapes by putting them onto the correct part of the Venn diagram.

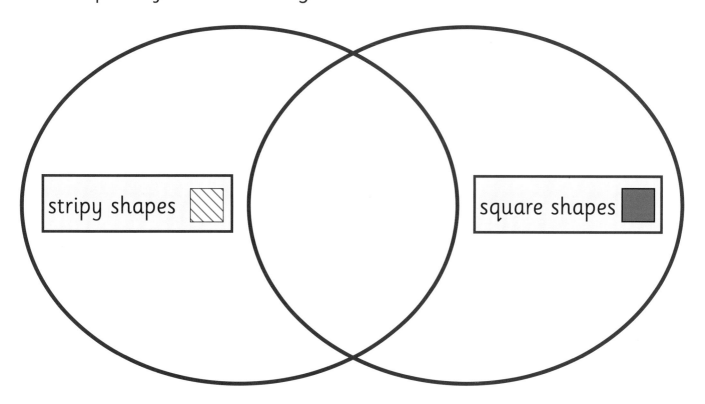

How many shapes are squares?

How many shapes are stripy?

How many stripy squares do you have?

50	20	40
80	70	10
100	30	90

Write the tens numbers in order.

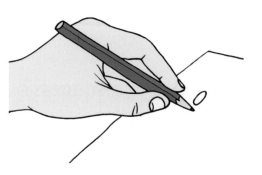

Start your list with 0.

Which tens number is missing?

The number factory

Vocabulary

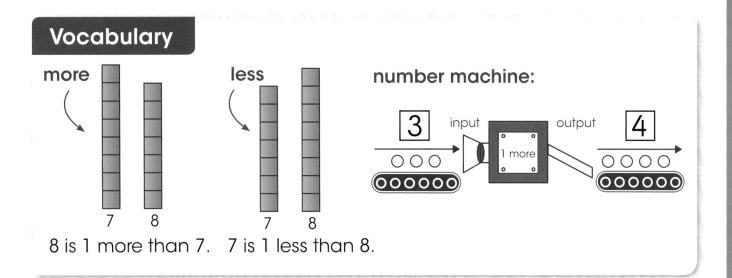

more

8 is 1 more than 7.

less

7 is 1 less than 8.

number machine:

input   output

3   1 more   4

Put these numbers into each machine.
What numbers come out?

10   25   30   17   4   14

Count on to find
more, count back
to find less.

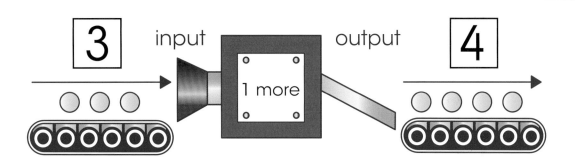

3   input   output   4

1 more

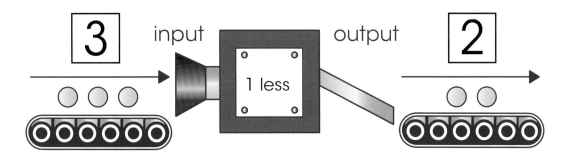

3   input   output   2

1 less

The number factory

Put these numbers into each machine.

10   25   30   17   4   14

What numbers come out?

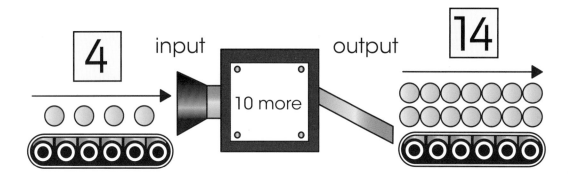

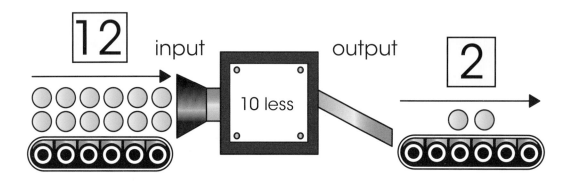

Tens and ones

How many different numbers can you make with tens and ones?

Use some arrow cards to help you.

Adding

Jamal ran out of time to complete these additions.
Ask your teacher for two number lines so that you
can help him to finish them.

Draw the jumps on
a number line.

12 +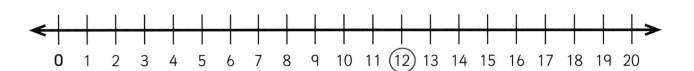

9 +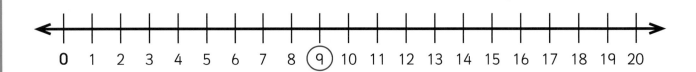

Addition

Add these numbers.

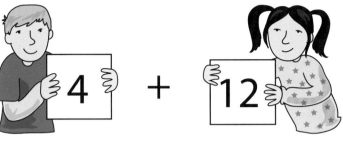 4 + 12

Think about which number to start with.

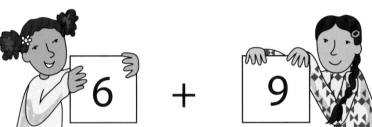 6 + 9

 10 + 5

 11 + 3

 9 + 9

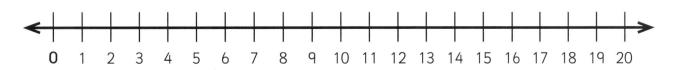

Subtracting

Sumi ran out of time to complete these subtractions.
Ask your teacher for two number lines so that you
can help her to finish them.

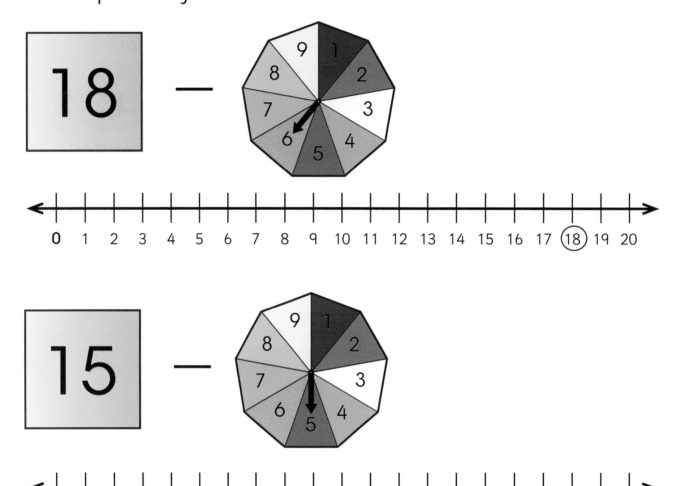

Draw the jumps on
a number line.

Equals

Which cards are equal?

3 + 5

6 + 3

7 + 3

9 + 3

4 + 4

4 + 3

8 + 2

2 + 5

5 + 4

6 + 1

2 + 4

3 + 3

7 + 1

5 + 7

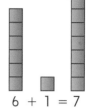

Find the total for each card first.

$6 + 3 = \boxed{9}$
$4 + 4 = 8$

Write the number pair sentences.

$4 + 3 = 7$ $6 + 1 = 7$
$4 + 3 = 6 + 1$

Broken number machine

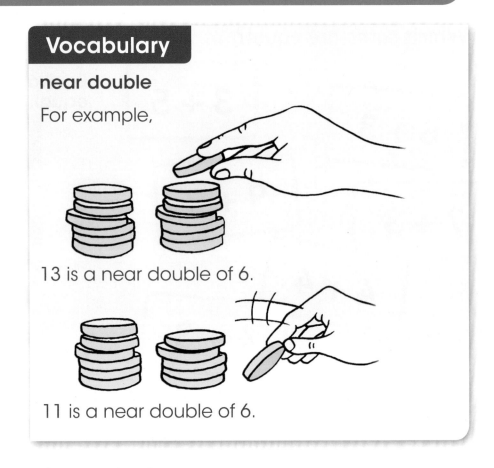

near double

For example,

13 is a near double of 6.

11 is a near double of 6.

Oh no! The number machine is broken.

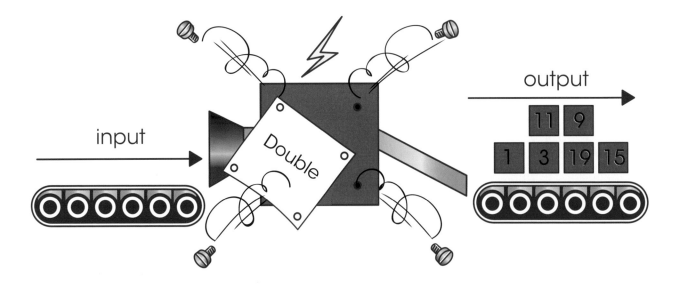

input

Double

output

11 9

1 3 19 15

What could the inputs have been?

Halves

Sibo is working out half of four.

Sibo is working out half of eight.

Put both hands in front of you with the same number of fingers raised on each hand. Then take one hand away. Now do the same for other numbers.

Can you work out half of two, half of six and half of ten in the same way?

Half a shape

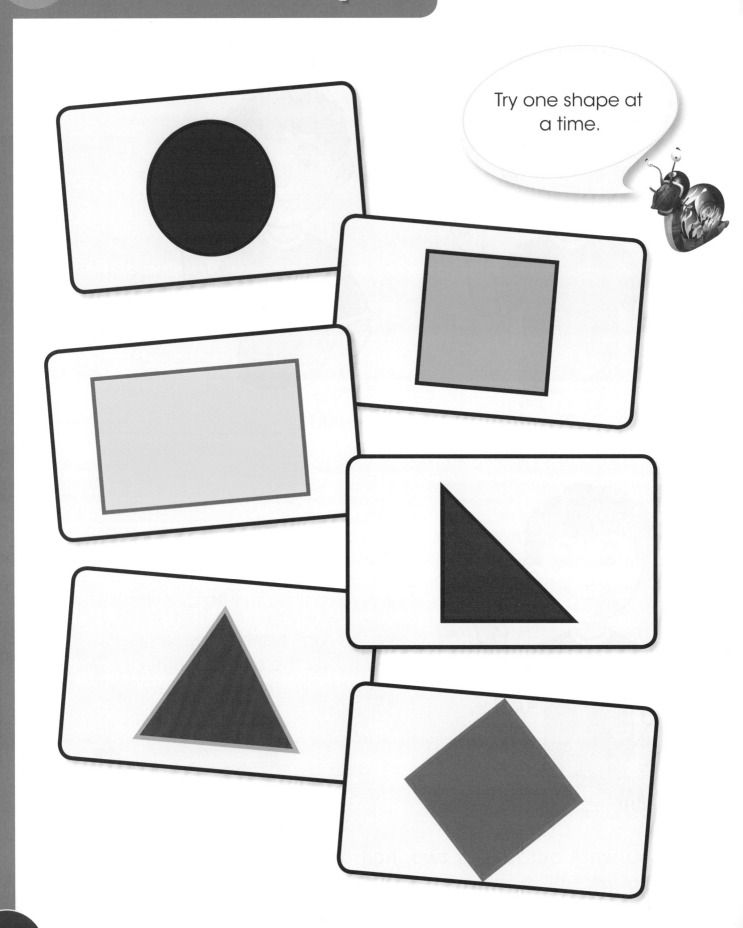

Try one shape at a time.

Sharing

Share the beads.

How many each?

Make sure the sharing is fair. The children must have the same number of beads each.

How many more?

How many more do you need to make a near ten?

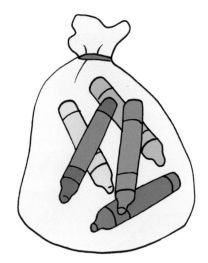

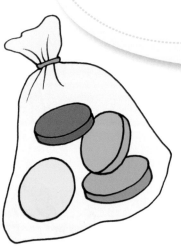

Use number pairs to ten to find out how many more are needed make ten. Then add one or find one less.

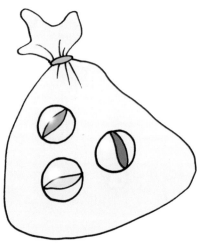

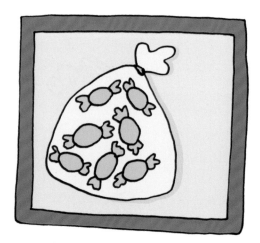

Subtraction check

Check each number sentence.
Is it correct?

What is missing?

Copy the number sentences.
Fill in the missing numbers.

Use counters to help you.

$$5 + \boxed{} = 12$$

$$\boxed{} + 7 = 11$$

$$\boxed{} + 6 = 18$$

$$4 + \boxed{} = 15$$

Money, money!

You will need:

money

a dish

a money dice

a purse each

What would you buy?

Caterpillars

How long is each caterpillar?

Make your own caterpillar.
How long is it?

Weight problems

The ball weighs nine cubes.

How many cubes do you think each toy will weigh?

Weight comparison

heavy   light

Where would you place these? Heavy or light?

Find more things to weigh.

Capacity

Find or make different containers.
What can you find out about their capacity?

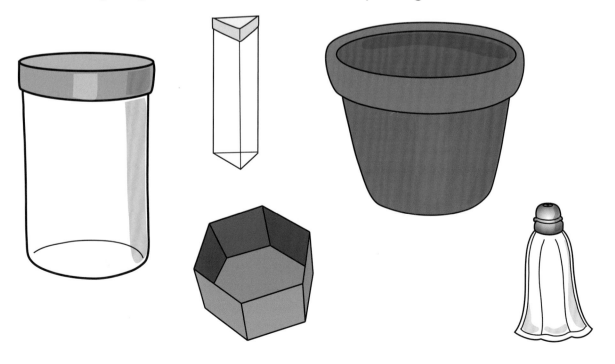

Which do you think has the biggest capacity?

Which do you think that has the smallest capacity?

Observing time

We get older as time passes.

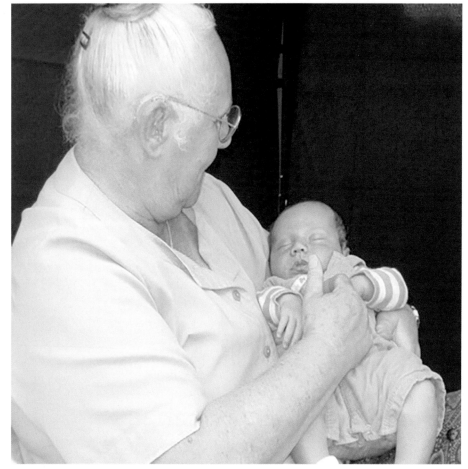

Clocks

one o'clock

two o'clock

three o'clock

four o'clock

five o'clock

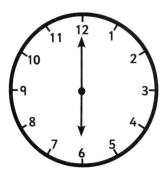

six o'clock

seven o'clock

eight o'clock

nine o'clock

ten o'clock

11 o'clock

12 o'clock

What time?

What do you do in a day?
You will need to think about what time you get up,
and what you do next.
Use the pictures to help you.

I get up at ? o'clock.

I eat breakfast at ? o'clock.

I play at ? o'clock.

I have lunch at ? o'clock.

Order of months

What order are the months of the year?

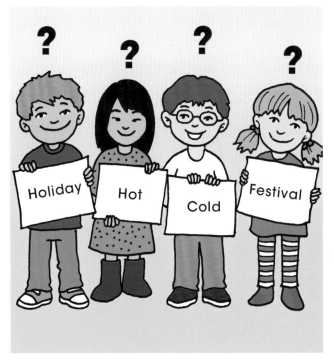

Describe each month of the year using one word.

Counting data

Class A were asked to pick their favourite meal time from

breakfast

lunch

dinner

This is the data that was collected.

How can you count the data?

How can you present the data?

Carroll diagram

Work with a friend to sort these shapes.

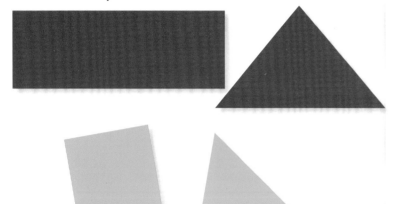

Vocabulary

carroll diagram:

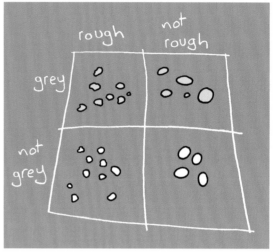

	red	not red
rectangle		
not rectangle		

Sorting Data

Alba wants to know what drinks to serve at sports day.

She finds some information from her class but it is not sorted. Represent the data any way you like.

José – juice

Alberta – Water

Eva – tea

Veronica – juice

Alejandra – juice

Belèn – water

Diego – juice

Sergio – tea

Jorgé – cola

Pablo – juice

Maria – tea

José - water

You can:

Sort the information into groups.

TEA	JUICE	
Maria, Serigo	Pablo, José	

Use a Venn diagram.

Hot drink

Cold drink

Use a Carroll diagram.

	girl	boy
hot drink		
cold drink		

Make a pictogram, block graph, or something else. You choose.

5
4
3
2
1

tea   water

What drinks should Alba serve at sports day?